House Beautiful

POOLS

The Editors of
House Beautiful

Text by
Christine Pittel

HEARST BOOKS | NEW YORK

Copyright © 2001 by Hearst Communications, Inc.

It is the policy of Hearst Books, recognizing the importance of preserving what has been written, to print the books we publish on acid-free paper, and we exert our best efforts to that end.

Library of Congress Cataloging-in-Publication Data

Pittel, Christine
    House beautiful pools / by the editors of
House Beautiful
        p. cm.
      isbn 1-58816-022-X
        1. Swimming pools. 2. Water gardens
I. House beautiful.
      II. Title.   III. Title: Pools.
      TH4763 .H59 2001
      728'.962—dc21   99-088582

cip

Printed in the United Kingdom

FIRST EDITION

1 2 3 4 5 6 7 8 9 10

Edited by Alanna Stang
Designed by Susi Oberhelman

Produced by Smallwood & Stewart, Inc., New York, NY

www.housebeautiful.com

CONTENTS

Foreword   9

Introduction   11

PART I   13

IN THE SWIM

From sculptural outdoor pools to indoor pools with all the splendor of a Roman bath: the swimming pool as the ultimate accessory for the home

PART II   61

GARDEN IDYLL

Ponds, fountains, reflecting pools, and the magical landscapes that surround them: the beauty of an oasis in the garden

PART III   119

POOLSIDE

Cabanas, decks, and patio furnishings: the relaxed pleasures of poolside entertaining and living

Directory of
Designers & Architects   169

Photography Credits   172

Foreword

No one flying across our great land can miss America's love affair with the swimming pool. Although water has played a strong role in architecture since Greek and Roman times, it is here, in the past century, that the swimming pool has come to reign in even modest suburban neighborhoods. As more architects, landscape architects, and designers create pools for their clients, we find they usually fall into one of two categories: Either they are designed as an extension of the house itself; or they become a feature of the larger landscape, placed some distance from the residence and its terraces and porches. And then some homeowners choose to build indoor pools to facilitate swimming as a part of their regimen year round.

Indoors and out, one growing phenomenon is the lap pool, in many ways easier to handle because of its smaller size, handsome proportions, and more tranquil use. Whatever the context, pools add up to a major enrichment of not only residential design, but of life itself. Whether conceived for a solitary swim or as a center of social life, the pool can be a major asset, as the projects in this handsome book attest. The poolside area is as important as the pool itself, of course, and one chapter focuses on ways to enhance this centerpiece of outdoor living. You will be amazed, and delighted, we hope, with the many moods that can be created around the pool. Writer Christine Pittel does an insightful job of describing the differences, enhancing the photographs taken for House Beautiful here and abroad. They are the heart of this book, just as the pools they reflect are often the heart of outdoor living today.

THE EDITORS OF
House Beautiful

Introduction

$\mathbb{B}$ ack when no one really knew what a swimming pool should look like, America's robber barons, who are credited with building the country's first pools, took their design cues from their own elaborate palm-lined parlors: Water simply replaced the Oriental carpets. Decades passed before these extravagant, marble-decked displays of Edwardian taste evolved into more streamlined backyard pools built on less exalted budgets. The suburbanization of America after World War II, the advent of pneumatically sprayed concrete, and a new health-oriented, outdoor lifestyle all democratized the pool, which became a smaller, simpler patch of water: Families that swim together stay together.

California was the launching pad for the new kind of pool, and Hollywood fueled its ascent with imagery and myth. It was the perfect cinematic setting; the camera loved its clean lines and aquatic colors, and audiences soaked up the walking, swimming Hollywood idols who embodied Greek ideals.

By the 1950s, middle-class homeowners were slipping through sliding glass doors into the largest of their rooms, the backyard, to spring off the diving board into turquoise waters. Notions of modern art had filtered into landscape design, and the yard behind tens of thousands of ranch houses became a grassy canvas of close-cut lawns and densely planted borders curving around kidney-shaped pools. A free and open garden plan replaced more formal designs inherited from Europe.

The pendulum of style swings even for the backyard. Today, homeowners prefer lap pools to ink drops. In areas with dense, deciduous plants and trees, designers propose naturalistic dark-bottomed pools, often intended for fish rather than people. There is more variety than ever before in a vibrant tradition now embarking on its second century.

Water has graced homes since antiquity, when the Greeks and the Romans turned gardens into realms of the senses. Classical landscape traditions, with ponds and fountains deliberately placed on the center axis in formal compositions, survived and evolved in Europe throughout the nineteenth century, while English gardeners

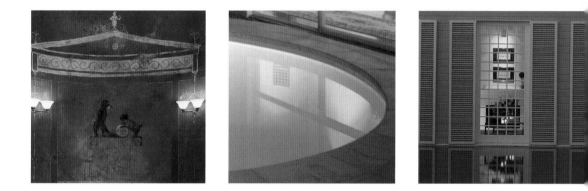

IN THE SWIM

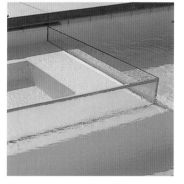

revolutionized the way people thought about how plants and water could relate to their settings. This century, that rethinking may have been less spectacular but perhaps more sweeping, as the terrain of invention shifted from estates and palaces to the suburbs, and expansive ideas intended for broad vistas telescoped into postage-stamp real estate.

Fortuitously, Frank Lloyd Wright was on the spot to reinvent the rapport between the newfangled suburban house and its surrounding yard. He was one of the first designers to rethink water's role in the emerging microcosm. The architect who broke the box inside also broke through box hedges outside, extending walls from the house into the garden. In this reconceived landscape, Wright eased reflecting pools into the lowest points of the site, where water would naturally collect. Fallingwater represents the most dramatic of his waterworks, in which house, landscape, stream, and natural pools fuse into a spectacular whole. But he also created more modest settings, using all the elements at the disposal of man and nature simultaneously—plants, terraces, walls, trees, light, views. After Wright, no pool was an island. Designers could associate water with architectural elements, incorporating pools within a house or next to its architectural offshoots in the garden. The juxtaposition of even a small body of water lends a house grandeur and serenity, suggesting a latter-day moat.

Wright's most familiar landscape was the prairie, and his yards, devoted to organic design, were intimate morality plays about nature. But many designers creating pools on sites with majestic views have transposed his ideas by playing with a larger panorama, lifting the water up into the view, letting it cascade over the edge to drop out of sight. Over the last two decades, technology has caught up with vision, and designers can now build an "infinity lip" that allows water to disappear over the thinnest of rims. If the pool overlooks an ocean, the pool's plane of water merges with the sea beyond to establish what appears to be a continuous surface, and a cosmic connection.

Some designers introvert rather than extrovert their pools for an effect that can be equally riveting. In the 1950s, the nationwide assumption was that a pool's bottom must be white, and the Polynesian results are still visible from planes flying overhead. But the more recent tendency has been to add varying amounts of gray or beige to deepen the color of the water, and to play with its natural chromatic variations. Some adventuresome souls have tiled or painted the pool's walls and bottom to create aqueous displays of color and pattern that are at once magnified, shifted, and blurred in its painterly depths.

Page 12: A contoured pool and kidney-shaped tiled deck add to the island imagery of a remodeled lakeside house in central Florida. Tampa architects Jan Abell and Kenneth Garcia created a "village" of white forms under a Caribbean roof scape, evoking the sunstruck languor of more exotic shores in a subdivision populated mostly by ranch houses. With a palm tree in the hollow of the pool's curve, and a wave pattern incising the house's stucco exterior, they transform the suburban scene into a tropical oasis.

Opposite: Ripples dissolve the blue-and-white zebra pattern lining a pool in San Miguel de Allende, north of Mexico City. The touch of an artisan's hand can be seen everywhere in this magical setting, from the pool and wall tiles—fabricated in the town of Dolores Hidalgo— to the variegated marble deck and carved stone column. The high walls of the town's fabled old mansions, reminders of a brisk silver trade in the eighteenth century, focus on the spaces within, intensifying the unexpected underwater graphics.

Window on the Pacific

The cinematic house Richard Neutra designed in 1938 for an MGM executive stood on a sliver of beachfront in Santa Monica until its current owners bought the vacant lot next door. They wanted extra space

In an echo of Richard Neutra's outdoor-oriented designs, wide glass walls at the near and far ends of the addition slide back into concrete pockets, opening both the original structure, above, and the new space, opposite, to the pool in an uninterrupted spatial sweep.

for entertaining guests, an informal family area, and room for the pool. Los Angeles architect Steven Ehrlich proposed an addition that would be party space, family room, and poolside cabana all in one. To minimize the addition's impact on the Neutra house (once owned by Mae West), the architect used a glass tunnel to separate the two structures. The semicircular bay window of the

An automatic stainless-steel gate, set into the white garden wall, rolls back to reveal a magnificent ocean vista, opposite. Below left, thick short walls of glass separate the spa from the lap lanes. "The glazed underwater enclosure lets the pool read as a pure rectangle," says the designer, who chose white plaster to complement the light palette of the surrounding scene.

original house (and perhaps Ms. West's silhouette!) inspired Ehrlich's vaulted roof, which sits on spider-leg columns that borrow from other Neutra designs.

The sleek addition presides over a new rectangular pool and reconfigured garden by landscape designer Barry Beer, who aligned the end of the pool with a sliding gate that opens to the sand and the Pacific beyond. A spa is tucked into a corner of the pool's shallow end. Discreetly set back on the new lot

behind the pool, the spa's glassy transparency poses little competition to Neutra's pristine white volumes.

In the best California tradition — merging outdoors and in — the concrete deck around the pool flows through the addition and out back to the garage, forming one continuous surface. The openness is possible because the high-perimeter walls endow the property with rare outdoor privacy, violated only by the palm-lined palisades above.

Next to the gate, behind a pivoting wall, a glass-tiled shower, above center, serves people coming in from the beach or the pool. Nearby, a pool cover slips unobtrusively under a metal lid. The carefully poured concrete walls and scored decking, above right, are treated with an acid wash to produce a light, elegant surface.

POOLS

Artful Oasis
in Santa Fe

One stroke short of being a full lap, the 13½-by-48-foot swimming pool was conceived as the focus of an outdoor family area geared to the grandchildren at the home of a contemporary art patron in the high desert near Santa Fe. The house, designed by architect

The pool stretches out in front of the entry to the house, above, bouncing western light off its shallow water onto the plain surfaces of the house's interior. Opposite, the architects paved the deck with limestone and kept all pool paraphernalia simple and serene. No detail detracts from the power of the abstract cubic masses.

J. D. Morrow and his former partner, Suby Bowden, forms an L around the pool and yard, which offers a cabana, kitchen, and tall, sheltering trees for informal living in the sun. Like the house, which is simplified to set off the art, the exterior is an extension of the gallery-like interiors, designed by interior architect Joe D'Urso and decorators James Aman and Anne Carson. The stark desert also cued the subdued, lean-lined aesthetic: The architects designed the concrete, adobe, and stucco house to frame the distant Ortiz Mountains. "The minimalism of the landscape plan suited the concept of the house, which does not depend on decoration," says Morrow. Rejecting the idea of a Santa Fe-style house, the client wanted a design that evoked local traditions without being literal. "The style is high modern, with regional design features that echo the architecture of the Southwest," Morrow adds. "The house opens to the landscape, which remains the main attraction—how can you compete with the mountains and the wildflowers?"

The architects created an optical "frame" with straight lines and natural colors so the subtleties of shape and texture in the landscape would become more legible. The limestone deck, poured-concrete walls, and gravel ground cover form a nearly monochromatic composition that brings out the hushed gradations of the desert.

Blue Sky Swim

Sometimes a pool belongs to the landscape beyond its confines. On a hillside in Sonoma County, California, San Francisco-based architects Turnbull Griffin Haesloop sited a pool to respond to the grandeur of the panorama. "The pool is tethered to two big landscape pictures at either end," says project architect Eric Haesloop. "On one side, you have a wide valley view, and at the other end, a rise with rock outcroppings; you're swimming in the space between those two elements." The architects used water to establish the relationship of the hillside to the valley below. A wood aqueduct with a copper lining conducts recirculated water from the rock outcropping to the pool as though from a spring to a pond via a waterfall. The height of the aqueduct guarantees a robust splashing sound "and a nice amount of sparkle from the sun for falling that far," says Haesloop. On the valley side, water cascades over a knife edge that brings the water and the sky together with reflections uninterrupted by any visible rim.

With the help of a chlorine-reducing filtering system, standard poolside decking was replaced by a grass terrace that provides a sense of coolness. Without flower borders, the expansive lawn heightens the rural feel of the farm-style house, which is sided in natural wood and roofed in standing-seam metal. A water spout that recalls old wooden gutters accentuates the architectural vernacular.

Sculptural Splash

The clean lines of the modernist house that Phoenix architect Jack DeBartolo Jr. built for himself in Paradise Valley, Arizona, reach into the front yard, where, at the end of a parterre of grass, he and landscape architect Steve Martino extended the grid to include a rectangular pool. Set against a high retaining wall—which

serves as a fence and a sculptural means of recirculating the water—the pool was designed with an underwater ledge along three sides to accommodate the DeBartolo grandchildren. The architects colored the pool's plaster walls gray to give its signature blue a rich, deep quality, and they eliminated the usual coping with a concrete deck that cantilevers slightly over the water's edge. The concrete platform originally meant for poolside lounging provided the perfect pedestal for a heroic steel sculpture.

The austere serenity of the high-walled pool is punctuated with dynamism by Gary Slater's abstract steel sunburst.

Saint Tropez Serenity

ae Aulenti collaborated with nature on this rugged stretch of the Côte d'Azur near St. Tropez. The Italian architect terraced the rocky terrain to create a buildable site, leaving intact a huge outcropping that became the centerpiece of a seaside villa.

Between the two wings of the cubic Italianate house, above left, four pairs of French doors open from the kitchen onto the central piazza: trellises break the intensity of the meridional sun. The view from the entry, above right, includes a cascade of terraces that lead the eye out to a nearby island. A freestanding wall, opposite, visually separates the contained waters of the pool from the expansive ocean beyond.

Two wings of the two-story house frame the stone in a courtyard that opens to the Mediterranean. Following the contours of the shore, Aulenti—working with landscape architect Pierre François—created half a dozen narrow plateaus at different levels. On a lower level of the sculpted hillside, she placed a long, narrow pool that brings the pleasures of the Mediterranean up to the house's civilized shores. A wood foot-

bridge spans the pool, allowing access from the lowest paved terrace to the gently contoured lawn, which is landscaped simply with grasses and indigenous vegetation. The sandy—blond marble covering the floors extends to the decks and stairs, creating an almost surreal visual quiet broken only by the eruption of crevassed rock that serves as a natural amphitheater for contemplating the pool and ocean beyond.

The azure pool belongs as much to the architecture as to the sea and the rocky hillside into which it is set. Softened by a local palette of plants, including olives, oleanders, sumacs, palms, and tamarisks at the terrace edges, left, the slender pool sits at the base of the broad, almost civic flight of steps that lead down from the house's courtyard, above.

Southern Comfort

One of architecture's more urbane prac-
titioners, Hugh Newell Jacobsen avoids
athletic-looking pools in favor of designs that
work with the landscape and house to form
an aesthetic whole. In the new town of
Windsor, Florida, on a parcel with zero lot-
line zoning that encourages introverted yards,
the Washington, D.C., architect stretched a
pool between the two-story living room and
an open two-story summer house out back.

Building on Vincent Scully's belief
that "architecture is memorable only when it
is irrational," Jacobsen programmed a certain
eccentricity into the house by liquefying the
usually solid central courtyard and bringing
water right up to the sills of the two buildings.
"Some people were nervous about having
water right next to the house," he says. But as
a result, sunlight reflects off the surface and
flickers on the walls and ceilings. The plane
of water, more moat than recreational pool,
lends the house the stature of a château, each
facade the mirror image of the other.

Jacobsen added gray to the pool's plaster surface because it interacts with the
water's turquoise, creating a cobalt dark
enough to reflect the bookend structures. He
also integrated sound into the composition
with two splashing lion's head fountains on
the summer pavilion that recirculate the
pool's water.

The high ceiling of the summer
pavilion, above, creates a chimney
effect that draws breezes across
the water through the open aper-
tures—a form of environmental
air-conditioning. Opposite, the deck
surface, which resembles classical
travertine, is really made of inexpensive Summer Stone, a precast
concrete paver. The trellised
roof shades an enclosed cutting
garden adjacent to the garage.

The symmetry of the house,
twin of the summer pavilion,
is doubled in the reflective
surface of the generously
proportioned swimming pool.
The two-story living room's
tall doors slide into adjacent
pockets, and operable
shutters admit breezes while
providing shade. Three
underwater lights placed on
the living room side of the
pool illuminate the basin
without producing the glare
of headlights aimed at the
house. In the interest of
reducing visual clutter, the
architect eliminated swimming
pool paraphernalia—diving
board, stainless-steel ladder,
curved coping—so that
the pool, both day and night,
reads as a watery carpet
linking front and back.

Take Two in Hollywood

Eight squares of what designer Brian Murphy calls putting greens, above, angle haphazardly around the side of the house from the swimming pool to the whirlpool area. A "lawn" of gravel planted with occasional tufts of native Southern California grasses keeps the landscaping minimal and low-maintenance. A hanging chain conducts rainwater down from the roof's galvanized-metal gutters. With a wire fence at the edge of the steep hillside embankment instead of the typical hedges and flower borders, the pool and gravel yard blend into the panorama for an uninterrupted view of the Los Angeles basin, opposite.

The kidney-shaped pool with the million-dollar view was already there when Brian Murphy remodeled and expanded a ranch-style tear-down in the Hollywood Hills. Though moss was prospering on its walls and the shape was out of fashion, he treated it as a found object whose beauty would spring back with proper grooming. He restored the pool's organic grace and Sunset Boulevard glamour by replastering and recoping it, exchanging tile for the existing brick trim, and keeping the original plaster lining white.

Then, using the pool as a visual centerpiece, Murphy wrapped the house around it. He extended the roof of the living room out over the coping to capture daylight bouncing off the water; the ripples cast a constant shimmer on the white ceilings inside. An arched roof echoes the curves of the pool, keeping the eye circling the yard and house, horizontally and vertically. A projecting sunscreen of expanded metal joins the barrel roof in giving the pool area a sense of enclosure while allowing views to the sky and affording the interiors protection from the high summer sun. The two-story living room complements the generous dimensions of the pool, where even the curves of the deliberately placed baby grand piano confirm the larger geometries.

The house is so close to the pool that its curved edge seems to pressure the two-story glass-curtain wall, forcing its way into the volume of the barnlike room, left. A skylight set into the exterior overhang lines up with interior skylights, blurring the distinction between outside and in. From the living room, the roof acts as a brow framing a view stretching to downtown Los Angeles. Gridded shadows from the glass-curtain wall, above, fall across a polished concrete floor that works with the low winter sun as a passive solar device for retaining heat.

Overleaf: The uplit ceiling conspires with the pool lighting to extend the vertical dimension of the backyard thirty feet, from pool bottom to rooftop.

Star Quality

Water in a pool acts as a magnifying lens, and garden designer Edward Huntsman-Trout, working with legendary Hollywood architect Paul Williams, was one of the few designers who played with its distortional effects on sub-aquatic imagery. Williams cultivated what he called "theatrical passages": By placing the veranda of a white pavilion over the deep end

Glorious, intricate, and labor-intensive, a tiled sun bursts, and then bursts again, amid a constellation of stars ringed by the signs of the zodiac. Below, stainless-steel handrails and curvaceous steps lead straight into the center of the sunburst.

A white and spacious pool pavilion, nearly modernist but still enamored of tradition, overlaps the coping of the curvilinear pool with black-tie urbanity, opposite. At certain times of the day, the sun hits the sunburst with all the panache of a Hollywood production.

of Huntsman-Trout's flamboyant, zodiac-patterned pool in Holmby Hills, he staged a scene for a camera waiting to roll. The ornamental bottom is composed of handpainted tiles that somehow reverse optical expectations, creating the illusion that the deep end is shallow and rising. People stepping into the pool soon realize what they always suspected, that they occupy the center of the firmament.

Modern Greek Drama

With Olympian connotations rather than Olympic dimensions, Jacobsen's black-bottomed pool, with a ringside view of Athens, displays a classical sense of balance and restraint, above. To keep the lines clean and to maximize the views, he used plate glass for the terrace railings, making them almost invisible. The marble deck and coping, opposite, were quarried from a nearby mountain, which is framed by the four-poster porch.

Overleaf: Cypress and sable palms, which love to grow in tight, dry places, enliven the pool's terrace.

Six hundred feet above the plains of Ithaca, with the Acropolis itself a neighbor in the sky, this rocky site high in the hills adjacent to Athens suggested a classicized house, garden, and pool to architect Hugh Newell Jacobsen. In a long concrete structure that steps six levels up a 45-degree slope, he reinvented the language of his professional forebears. Known for his modernist interpretations of local architecture, Jacobsen poured concrete into cylinders to create columns with a more contemporary flute than their classical counterparts. By forgoing the traditional acanthus leaves and scrolls, he allowed abstract forms to emerge.

Between the lowest and the highest points of the house, Jacobsen positioned a wide outdoor deck and then carved out a classically proportioned black-bottomed pool. "The darker color makes it register more as a reflecting pool than as an exercise space," says the architect, who kept the design simple, specifying a pure rectangle with crisp edges and white marble coping. Landscaping is minimal and contained within planters and squared beds, suggesting the rationalism of a man-made environment rather than an evocation of nature. At the edge of the terrace, a colonnade with a continuous concrete lintel shades an outdoor seating area suitable for Zeus.

Sunscreens

|H|ouses designed in traditional architectural styles are often ill-equipped for poolside living under the blazing sun. Remodeling a gabled, two-story house in Sarasota, Florida, Benjamin Baldwin opened the closed forms of the conventional structure to the exterior and the swimming pool out back. The architect, a modernist known for his quiet touch, re-invented the boxy interiors to create flowing,

Straightforward and unsentimental, the deck around the pool, above and right, is as understated and elegant as Baldwin's interior design. The white tile rim of the pool incandesces in the sun, creating a corona of rippling light at the water's edge.

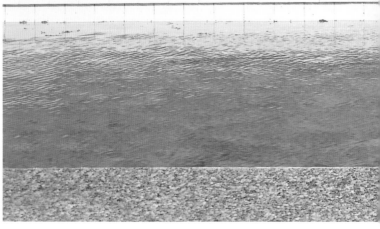

clean-lined spaces, some two stories tall. He took special care in the interface between the rear facade and the backyard, applying a latticed grill that works like an architectural veil, protecting the rooms and porches from the full blast of the sun. Then he carried the pebbled, slip-resistant deck surrounding the pool past the covered porch into a screened lanai that houses a small reflecting pool and a built-in barbecue. The garden is walled with tall hedges that channel the view from the house past the pool and back lawn to the bay beyond.

With portable chaise longues, left, Baldwin rolls the out-of-doors into the covered, screened lanai. A reflecting pool is centered on a modest jet of water, and a fan above the seating area assists with airflow on days when breezes fail. The same gray-stained trellis that screens the back balcony forms the walls of a dining gazebo, above, offering a shady refuge from the relentless Sarasota sun.

Following the Red Brick Road

D eprived of a pool in his Manhattan co-op, architect Leslie Armstrong's client—an industrial designer and collector of sculpture who specializes in ancient classical pieces—commissioned an indoor pool for his upstate New York country house as part of an addition that

The living room pavilion, furnished with Mies van der Rohe chairs, above, is separated from the pool area by glass walls that confine the humidity and allow zoned heating and ventilation. On the other side of the pool, right, natural light can be regulated by see-through scrims that drop over a wall of glass.

would include a guest room and living/dining pavilion. To prevent the sheer size of the new structure from overwhelming the existing house, Armstrong separated the two with a long glass causeway—a "glazed umbilical cord," she calls it. The elements of the new structure are visually linked by another kind of path: a red-tiled promenade that extends from the living room pavilion all the way out to a walled garden and beyond to the pool.

Nine degrees off the geometry of the pavilion, the pool creates decks of different sizes, left, for seating and sculpture. The gabled roof lends the room stature, and the plate-glass windows endow it with abundant light. Above, a working fireplace occupies a wall at the head of the pool, countering the presence of water with fire.

Treetop Vista

For an active Connecticut couple who wanted to swim daily, architect Jeffrey Mose designed an elevated structure with a suspended indoor lap pool. The sleek building, set on piers, looks like a covered bridge; inside, the Y-shaped steel columns and trusses echo the exposed heavy timber beams of the main house, which was assembled from old barns transported to the site. Large windows and a neutral interior palette create a serene space that defers to the treetops.

A sequence of plate-glass windows set into the steel framework, above, affords views of a river that runs through the property. To keep condensation from clouding the vista, the architect used linear diffusers in the stucco wall, which maintain air flow and balance the humidity. A thermal break in the aluminum frames supporting the glass, left, keeps the windows from fogging.

Roman Luxe

The client had two images in mind when he asked David Birn, a designer based in Cold Spring, New York, to create an indoor spa: one was the voluminous space of an old barn on his rural Quebec site; the other was Pompeii. Drawing on his experience as a set designer for the opera, Birn distilled the disparate referents into a vaulted, proscenium-like chamber dramatically centered on a whirlpool just large enough for in-place swimming against a water jet. He conceived of the space as "a spiritual room for the mind—cozy, dark, meditative," he says; but, in the best of Roman traditions, he designed the spa to stimulate the body as well, with a fully equipped adjacent gym. On the Pompeian-red walls are whimsical murals and Greek key-pattern mosaic trim. The effect of 2,100 years of decay was achieved by applying and removing plastic sheeting from joint compound spread over the walls, and then coloring the distressed surface with a combination of paints and rice paper.

The monumental pool is 3½ feet deep and made of prefabricated fiberglass, with steps that function as seats. Italian artisans living in Quebec installed mosaic bands in the marble decking and around the columns and cornices, adding authenticity to the freshly antiquated space.

59

Water is often the life of a garden, a reservoir that reflects the sky and surrounding vegetation. Yet it need not dominate the property or look like an empty vat when there's no one swimming in it. "The challenge of a pool in any setting," says Memphis landscape architect Ben Page, "is not to overwhelm the landscape with a blue hole."

GARDEN IDYLL

Once the *ne plus ultra* status symbol of home ownership, pools were conceived as the gems of their yards, set off with decks, grass, and border plantings in ever widening ripples that confirmed their central importance. Beautiful, organically shaped pools fashioned by California landscape architect Thomas Church in the late

1940s epitomized modernist designs that featured the pool and its sinuous contours while marginalizing the rest of the garden. Abstract sculpture literally rising from the depths of Church's expansive waters underscored the conceptual debt to modern art, and the Henry Moore-esque forms occupied the blue void. Even without swimmers, the pool in its landscape stood as an artistic composition writ in water.

Church's organic shapes were widely copied—and ultimately banalized in cookie-cutter builder designs that never had the budget for a centerpiece sculpture. In the 1970s, with the rise of historicist postmodernism in architecture, the minimally landscaped modern garden with its vacant bull's-eye was reconsidered. Landscape design became more complex and often more traditional, organized with strong axes and symmetries; pools themselves lost their autonomy as they became part of a more structured landscape. Gardens were conceived as suites of outdoor rooms rather than as free-flowing open space, and the pool, which was often fenced because of code requirements, became one feature among others. No longer an entity in itself, the pool functioned within a larger context, sometimes with rills running off to other basins, giving the gardens a backbone of water. The yard became a garden with a pool rather than a pool with a garden.

Impossible to reposition and too expensive to rebuild, pools are immovable objects that pose design problems for new homeowners who no longer appreciate an aesthetic that's two or three generations old. Confronted with a found object, owners have discovered that the best way to change the pool is to relandscape its surroundings. Often, part of the concrete deck is removed and the landscape brought nearer to link the garden and the water more directly. Or the landscape may run visual interference, baffling views so that the whole pool cannot be seen at one time from a single vantage point but, rather, is discovered in increments as strollers progress through discrete parts of the garden. An active landscape encourages pools with more modest dimensions and varying functions. The purpose may no longer be athletic but decorative—the water intended for contemplation, lily pads, and delight.

Page 60: Cherubs frolicking under cascading water imply that the basin is merely a fountain. But the nineteenth-century English stone sculpture is really a conceptual decoy, standing in the middle of a circular black-bottomed pool forty feet across. Suitable for swimming, the basin—one of a half dozen different ponds dotted across the grounds of a seventy-two-acre estate in Bucks County, Pennsylvania, owned by New York floral designer Renny Reynolds—is the focus of a much larger garden scheme. The water-spouting sculpture is centered on a wide swath of lawn that sweeps up to a temple-like structure.

Opposite: In his own backyard, Memphis landscape architect Ben Page created a sequence of outdoor rooms that entice the eye from one space to the next. Florence's garden, named after his daughter, is centered on a split-level pond surrounded by a deck of Tennessee crab-orchard stone. In the upper pond a pencil-thin fountain spurts from a single jet; the U-shaped fish pond below catches the overflow. "It's a play of exotic aquatic plant textures—rare tropical water lilies and papyrus," says Page. "I wanted to create an intimate seating area focused on the cooling aspects of water and sound."

Box Hedge Beauties

Necessity was the mother of reinvention for Memphis landscape architect Ben Page. In a garden on the side of a hill, the only terrain flat enough for a sixty-foot-long lap pool was right outside the sunroom of the 1920s Georgian house. Page had to devise a strategy to mitigate the pool's impact on the space and

As in formal European gardens, the pool conforms to the geometry radiating from the symmetry of the house. Where the pool widens to a conventional size, right, the brick paving that was inspired by the facade cedes to a deck of crab-orchard stone intended for lounging and poolside chairs. Sculpted topiary, above, rounds out the angular shrubbery.

the view from the house. Opting for a sophisticated sleight of hand, he designed his version of a French canal pool with formal landscaping on either side. The central bay of the sunroom aligns with the main axis of the pool, but from any other viewpoint the eye glimpses only part of the water. Page achieved this illusion using parterres planted with clipped box hedges that alternately pinch and release the sides, creating watery "rooms." Energetic bathers can swim straight down the middle and rack up laps, while others can meander from room to room within the pool.

From the lowest terrace, above, which is planted in a sophisticated perennial border, the view toward the pool includes box hedges, tardiva hydrangeas, and the terraced hillside beyond. Adjacent to the sunroom is a "sitting room," left, with an underwater banquette that rings the alcove before it necks down into the six-foot-wide swimming channel.

Next to Nature

Unlike many Romantics in the world of land-scape, garden designer George Schoellkopf believes in geometry and man-made spaces carved from nature. "The garden can be lazier and freer because the structure will hold it all together," he says. "If the garden is more free-form, the plants have to do more work." On the sloping grounds of his own farmhouse in northwestern Connecticut, he improved on nature by breaking vistas "to avoid having a grand sequence of spaces, and to make it all a little more mysterious and exciting." In this garden of delights and surprises, Schoellkopf sited a swimming pool—which is supplied and flushed by a gravity-fed jet from a stream—in such a way that visitors are compelled to walk through the garden and appreciate its features. Then he placed a small basin midway between the pool and a pond that invites a refreshing summer dip. The rectangle may not be the most naturalistic shape, but the basin—one edge of which exuberantly overflows with tobacco flowers, irises, and annuals—seems to be a man-made form reverting to nature.

To create the illusion of a pond that doesn't look vacant when no one is swimming in it, Schoellkopf painted its walls black and included a reed-like fountain at one end. He also detailed the deck so that no drains, lights, or filters disturb the bucolic reverie.

Caribbean Fantasy

hen he first saw it, garden designer Hitch Lyman was far from enthusiastic about his clients' kidney-shaped California-style pool; he felt it was out of place in a New York suburb. But they balked when he suggested

Turquoise waters conspire with tropical plantings and plants that merely look tropical—cut-leaf sumac, ailanthus, aralia, empress tree, and elderberry—to create what is, for the Northeast, a fantasy environment. Larger plants are concentrated near the pool's edge, above, where their big, dark leaves make a strong visual impact. Nearly hidden, the Caribbean-style changing room, opposite, provides a charming counterpoint to the curvilinear pool.

removing it, and counterproposed that they eliminate the concrete around the pool and bring the grass right up to the coping. Lyman agreed; then, taking his cue from a book on Caribbean architecture, he gave the pool's exotic shape and lagoon-blue hue a new context by landscaping the surrounding yard with tropical plants rather than with the existing junipers and birches.

"There was this terrible little garden shed that had not been painted in twenty years, and we decided to turn it into a

Jamaican house," Lyman recalls. By converting the shed into a changing room and painting its facade bright shades of blue, pink, and white, the architect created a visual echo of the pool's color and a functional centerpiece for the garden's new, unexpected theme. To relieve the drudgery of bedding out real tropicals every spring, he imported faux-tropicals—hearty plants with luxuriant foliage—then followed that inva-

sion with a profusion of bananas and cannas, and about one hundred elephant's-ears. Chartreuse helichrysum and white lamium introduced lime green and white into the color scheme, and nasturtiums provided flashes of red and orange. "All we were doing was trying to take the curse off a bad piece of 1950s design," notes Lyman. "It wasn't meant to be serious or permanent, just amusing."

Above center, a banana tree and a cluster of elephant's-ears stand sentinel over the pool, their leaves drooping toward the water.

Page 72: Flowering spots of exotic hues match the intense colors of the pool and the cabana — a welcome surprise in the middle of a forest glade.

Secret Garden

he upstate New York hideaway of early-twentieth-century garden author Louise Beebe Wilder (who was also a gifted garden designer and often collaborated with Stanford White) was derelict but enchanting when New York designer David Easton first saw it. Toppled concrete columns—relics of a long-ago pergola—surrounded what had once been a colonnaded yard, but they still suggested the original garden layout, a large rectangular enclosure several steps down. "You knew it had been a garden but weren't sure of the exact details," says Nancy Goslee Power, a California landscape designer who had read Wilder's books and advised Easton and James Steinmeyer, his partner in the restoration. In the lawn of the sunken garden, Easton sited a small ten-by-twenty-foot pool, in keeping with

In the beds and borders around the pool, landscape designer Nancy Goslee Power's strategy was to mix rather than separate flowers, planting each variety in bunches to give a sense of fullness. "I tend to overplant because I want that impression of fullness," she says. With wisteria growing over the pergola and climbing roses covering the cottage's white trellises, the effect is "overgrown and rampant."

the original scale of both the cottage and the garden. "When you're not jumping in for a quick dunk, it works as a reflecting pool," says Power, "which makes good sense, since you spend more time looking at a pool than swimming in it." Fieldstone walls were rebuilt around the inner courtyards and flower beds were resurrected as borders for the paths and fringes for the grass carpet.

For designer David Easton, a porch is a magical in-between place, simultaneously an indoor and outdoor area. He has furnished the long, sheltered space between his house and garden, left, as if it were an actual room, with lamps, rattan furniture, trophy china, and a wooden deer's head with real antlers. Under the pergola, above, a pair of crisp white lawn chairs bring the focus of the garden back to its centerpiece, the pool.

Plain and Simple

In order to establish a minimalist yard to match the minimalist house he designed for a Dallas client, Lionel Morrison wiped the slate green. He carpeted the space with an expanse of grass, within which he placed two concrete pads side by side to create an axis parallel to the long house. In one of the concrete squares, he centered an eight-by-eight-foot spa; in the other, he set a table for spa-side dining. To emphasize the formality of the outdoor composition, two trees were symmetrically planted on either side of the shallow stairs that step up to the low plinth on which the house rests. Without decorative flower borders blurring the edges, the geometric structure of the garden is as definitive as the spare, uncluttered interiors, where furniture is kept away from the walls to augment the sense of open space.

The landscape design is cast in the same abstract language as the house. Architect Lionel Morrison restricted the palette of plant materials, endowing the space with a clean-lined asceticism, and chose concrete pads for low-maintenance decking. The collar immediately arround the spa can be used for casual sitting or sunbathing, and the adjacent square can accommodate sit-down entertaining and dining.

Pool with a View

Lynn von Kersting, co-owner and interior designer of the Ivy, a well-known Hollywood restaurant, converted a dormant garden into an Eden of family activity featuring an existing pool and a spectacular view of Los Angeles. She added an outdoor fireplace with a wood-burning oven and planted herbs and citrus and olive trees, showing how the California concept of the working garden proliferates the reasons—and expands the season—for living outside.

Lynn von Kersting created a sense of abundance around the pool and guesthouse, left, with hundreds of sweet-smelling roses, rampant morning glory vines, and a profusion of rosemary and lavender. Camellias and gardenias add fragrance to the romantic overgrowth, which looks as though it has been flourishing effortlessly for years. Hanging pots of Tuscan geraniums, above, range over the pool-house walls.

Moroccan Paradise

ater gives the Marrakech garden of Elie Mouyal both its magic and its structure. "The Arab garden is a transposition of the image of paradise, but we imagine paradise to be very organized and rational," he says. The

Mouyal transformed and enlarged what was the original entry of an agricultural building into a garden porch, above left and right, with an intricately carved arch he transported from another garden. Doubling as an outdoor room where meals are sometimes served, the scallop-edged pavilion locks into the geometry of the garden with a primary arch centered on one of the farm's main canals, right.

Paris-trained architect explains that because water is precious in his culture, having, holding, and distributing it constitutes the primary theme and pleasure of Arab gardens. Mouyal has spent six years developing the pools and canals of an old farm in an ancient palm oasis where he turned a nearly ruined agricultural structure into a home. The story of the garden is the story of its water, which—for purposes of irrigation—starts in a corner of the site at the highest point, in a large, shallow holding

pond that doubles as a reflecting basin and swimming pool. Mouyal respected the existing pattern of irrigation ditches; his interventions have been cautious and subtle, simply making the canals permanent by anchoring them in rock and concrete. Water spills over the lip of the holding tank into troughs that feed a network of canals, which flow past olive trees, palms, and flower beds. Despite their beauty, Arab gardens are working enclaves intended to produce fruit, vegetables, and herbs, but Mouyal calls his five acres "a farm operetta"— more of a stage set exemplifying the principles, but not the productivity, of a working garden.

Fed by gravity from an irrigation basin at the highest point in the garden, a rock-and-concrete canal, above, acts as a stream watering linear beds of roses on both sides. The canal passes by the back of the house, where olive trees frame an outdoor terrace just beyond the living room and palm trunks act as columns supporting woven reed shades, left.

An expansive retaining basin, filled with motor-pumped water from a well beneath the trellised pergola, left, is the source of water for the entire five-acre farm. Water spills over one edge and down a short flight of steps into a secondary basin, above; this, in turn, supplies the farm's network of irrigation canals. The interior walls of the concrete pool are painted black, turning the surface into a palm-reflecting mirror.

Tropical Showcase

The standard-issue 1950s builder's pool that landscape architect Raymond Jungles and artist Debra Yates got with their Florida house was definitely biomorphic: "If not a kidney, some other unidentifiable internal organ had to be the model," says Jungles, who replaced "a lot of junk vegetation" with show-stopping tropicals. Jungles retiled the pool's edges and

Between the concrete paving squares, downy zoysia grass softens the edges of the landscape, below left. Next to the silver palm, a stand of golden Hawaiian bamboos, below right, ties the garden into the yellows of a mosaic mural.

Jungles chose an array of tropical plants—heliconia, fishtail palm, yellow walking iris, and bromeliad —to echo the sinuous lines of the pool. At the shallow end, opposite, a silver palm promises to shade the sun-stroked water.

recoated the plaster lining silver gray so that the water would take on the "color of the sky." Behind the pool, he layered a set of handcrafted walls; the front one features an abstract geometric composition of smashed tiles designed by Yates. The mural's energetic shapes and vivid colors play off the pool's abstract curves.

Perspective Cubed

Outside, the style of the new addition is traditional, but inside its lines are clean, crisp, and contemporary. Structural piers mirrored on the surface of the new indoor pool, above, frame a view into the garden. They initiate a long perpendicular axis that runs through the center of a borderless canal, up a flight of terraced steps, and to a lawn centered on the original swimming pool, opposite.

W hen the owners of an estate in Limburg, Belgium, commissioned an indoor pool as part of a contemporary annex to a traditional country house, they were willing to give up the existing outdoor pool. Belgian father-and-son landscape architects Jacques and Peter Wirtz decided to use the old pool as part of a new plan to link the garden to the house. The scheme included a newly acquired neighboring property, which had been a working nursery crossed by roadways lined with trees.

The designers, who specialize in formal gardens tempered by intimate pockets, transformed the old stone-rimmed pool into a lily pond and brought it visually closer to the house with a short flight of shallow steps. Water from the pond cascades to a grass-edged canal in a sunken garden. Beyond the pool, another pond, dense with aquatic plants, extends the axis of water deeply into the landscape through a narrow pass of beech hedges, where major allées of the former nursery sweep unexpectedly to the right. "The straight view is deflected into a diagonal, creating a very dynamic feeling," says the younger Wirtz. Out of view, behind an ivy-draped garden pavilion to the right of the old pool, lies a series of beds with roses, ornamental shrubs, and vegetables where the monumental garden gets intimate.

A series of watery terraces, walled in with high hedges, form a composition of cubic volumes that leads the eye into the depths of the garden through a structured sequence of openings.

Follow the Water

In a compound overlooking the Pacific, water provides a sensuous link between two modernist houses. A narrow canal, designed by Marc Fisher while in the office of landscape architect Emmet I. Wempel, wends its way from the parking area past a Case Study House by Charles Eames and Eero Saarinen, to a set of stairs, where it cascades over a small weir that appears to feed a lap pool. After the weir, the runnel disappears under a terrace, reappearing behind a new two-story house by architect Barry Berkus. It then vanishes again, only to resurface in its endpoint, a pool next to the front door.

Planes of water mix with stone terraces and acid-washed concrete walls to form abstract ground patterns. Lined with river stone and raked with underwater lighting, the runnel, left, is illuminated so that its ripples refract the shimmering play of light. The lap pool's floor, above, is tinted the color of sand so that its turquoise water recalls the hues of the Pacific beyond.

Gothic Folly

ep Durenberger was left with an archae-ological dig—a gaping basement and an underground cistern—after he moved the house next door to annex its 50-by-150-foot lot for a garden. For most people, the remains of the house might simply be holes in the ground to be filled in, but the retired antiques dealer and lifelong gardener treated the remnants as assets that would give his plain plot on the Midwest prairie a third dimension. He transformed the old cistern into a goldfish pond by simply raising its floor several feet and adding a fountain urn. He then landscaped part of the former base-ment into a deep pool of greenery. Over the far part of the basement, he built a two-story fantasy lookout that he calls a covered bridge. The wooden structure, which arches over a grotto, includes a comfortably fur-nished outdoor room that opens onto a view of the sunken garden and cistern.

A nineteenth-century copy of a dwarf, originally carved in Italy during the Renaissance, presides over a diminutive fountain that enlivens the shal-low fishpond. Durenberger's characteristic use of local materials—"nothing rare and demanding"—applies to the plants, the common gravel used on the garden paths, and the pond, which is edged with local Kasota stone.

H O U S E   B E A U T I F U L

The fishpond plays a pivotal geometric role in the garden's layout, marking the center point of an axis that stretches from the side porch of the 1859 house to a clearing centered on a statue. Durenberger took a second axis

The cross axis of the garden starts at the two-story wooden folly, above left, and terminates at the "chapel," above right. Garden structures and hedges mask views, define precincts, and draw the eye to focal points like the pool, the Gothic window, or the carved marble lion's head that appears to feed a basin in the sunken garden, opposite.

that starts at the covered bridge and extended it toward the back of the lot, where a pergola built in forced perspective leads to a "chapel," its window gothicized with strips of willow. A cedar shrub beyond the window opening, and a mirror hanging on the back fence enhances the illusion of perspectival depth. "It's a small garden in a simple village," says Durenberger. "We tried to be playful and not get too serious on the half-acre lot."

In the French Manner

hree meters belowground on the scorched twenty-five-acre farm they bought outside Avignon, Dominique Lalande and Bruno Lafourcade discovered water. The couple— she is a landscape designer, he is an architect —exploited and featured it as the most evocative element in their new garden. With the

Lalande positioned a stone sphere, above, amid similarly shaped topiary around the pond. A new basin, right, made from the concrete foundation of a former sheepfold, reflects the turn-of-the-century farmhouse and its venerable plane trees.

help of a wind-driven pump, they drew the water from the earth into a wide basin fronting the house and stocked it with lilies, papyruses, and fish. Its overflow pours into a canal that leads to a pond. "The water attracts ducks, herons, and frogs," says Lalande. "There's a whole life right there, a ballet on water, a permanent spectacle that's equally intriguing to kids and adults."

Lalande laid out the garden symmetrically around the geometry of the water, within

At the end of the canal, a topiary wreath, opposite, centers on a dangling mirrored sphere that reflects sunlight and moonlight back to the house. Lalande uses hedges everywhere to protect her beloved iris and lavender, below left.

In the shallow reflecting basin, a rowboat, above right, allows people to float amid the flora and fauna of the pond's living menagerie.

the larger right-angled organization of the neighboring farms. In Provence, farmers wall their orchards and fields with densely planted cypress hedges to protect them from the insistent mistral winds. "I aligned everything in the garden to work with the cypress, to stay in harmony with the landscape," says Lalande.

California Dreamin'

At a Montecito house, garden designer Nancy Goslee Power enclosed the entire yard, front and back, with stuccoed walls and dense hedges, transforming it into a protected space where the house can open freely, without loss of privacy. Within the garden, she used bright rosemary to rim a series of outdoor rooms, including one centered on a frog pond just

inside the front gate. Straight lines and rectangular plans give the garden structure; naturalistic plantings soften the lines. Mediterranean and California perennials—phlomis fruiticosa, Santa Barbara daisy, angel's-trumpet—form a "California border" of plants that do well in the arid climate.

A stalwart frog presides over a small fishpond, left. Peppermint-scented geranium wraps the shoulder of a garden bench like a cowl, above.

Gentleman's Retreat

nterior designer to British nobility, David Hicks was an architect of water at the Grove, his own country estate in Oxfordshire. When he moved there with his wife in 1980, the property was hardly more than a farm, but he rapidly transformed the landscape with a

highly structured plan in which water plays a principal role. The swimming pool, the primary aquatic feature on the property, is subsumed, Louis XIV style, within an avenue of chestnut trees radiating axially from the house. The vista is framed by the dining room windows, which direct the sight lines.

At the end of his posthumously published book, *My Kind of Garden*, Hicks lists among his pet peeves "turquoise swimming pools," so when he built his long, slender

"Position is everything in garden design," said Hicks, who centered a long, narrow swimming pool in the symmetrical vista extending from the dining room window, above left. Naturalized by its stone borders and devoid of deck furniture and athletic props, the gentleman's pool, above right and opposite, bears a strong resemblance to its distant ancestor in formal European gardens, the basin.

Chief among the garden follies in Hicks's landscape is a crenellated tower, opposite, its three-sided moat spanned by a drawbridge and covered with waterlilies in summer. The view from the tower, below center, reveals a wall of horn-beam trees and hedges behind two slabs of clipped hawthorne, each pierced by sprays of artichokes in plastic pots.

bathing basin, he made sure its surfaces were painted black. That way "it does not look like a heated, filtered pool; it looks like a formal piece of water," he wrote.

In 1990, on another part of the estate, his wife built a tower pavilion as his sixtieth birthday gift. Hicks surrounded the turreted station with a moat on three sides, and when the sought-after designer needed a retreat, he crossed the water, raised the drawbridge, and took up residence in the tower, which is

adjacent to a secret walled garden filled with peonies, foxgloves, lilies, salvias, and old roses.

Hicks's pools and ponds always conformed to the straight-line geometries he preferred, reinforcing a larger, clearly ordered picture that frequently took direct aim at the horizon. "Symmetry was his thing," says his son, Ashley. "Vistas everywhere."

Goldfish, above left, sun themselves in a basin refreshed by water arching from a small stone pyramid. At the end of a garden axis, above right, where two lawn chairs are poised for a restful pause, water brims over an urn into a brick fountain.

Renaissance on the Riviera

om Parr, the former chairman of the renowned London decorating firm Colefax & Fowler, presided over the interiors of the Renaissance-style villa on the French Riviera, while retired businessman Claus Scheinert took charge of the gardens of their manse (which is a copy of Madame de Pompadour's pavilion at Fontainebleau). In tackling the neglected grounds, Scheinert—who had never planted so much as a petunia before—was taking over a former jasmine farm whose twelve terraces were over grown with weeds, unkempt cypress hedges, and shapeless cherry laurels.

An early decision to fill in an existing swimming pool that crowded the classically detailed house liberated the water from its

Configured on a short jet of water, a new circular koi pond with eighteenth-century coping graces a terrace under the arching brow of the ocher villa. Calla lilies, papyruses, and potted irises can be removed from the shallow water. Blue plumbago, with its lacy mass of light-blue flowers, also grows in the movable pots of a portable landscape surrounding the pond.

tight domestic confines. Scheinert meta-morphosed the conventional pool into a stone-rimmed pond, lowering it to an adjacent terrace and centering it in a landscaped outdoor room. "It's not a pool where anyone swims," he says. "Now we can look down on it." The self-taught designer planted and groomed nearly a dozen hillside terraces in what has been, since 1984, a long, loving work in progress. He favored a flower palette of soft blues, pale whites, and cloudy lavenders, colors that blend into continuous drifts. The result is a lush, hauntingly atmospheric garden that is both formal and informal: The exuberance of the plantings blurs the underlying geometry of circles and squares, interspersed among stately, architectural allées. "With these terraces, the bones were already there—what was difficult was to forge a unity from it all," says Scheinert. Water provides a consistent theme and constant pleasure, running all through the garden from pond to rill to cistern. "Every garden in a hot climate should have water," he says. "The sound of the splashing makes you feel cool."

Water from the gaping mouth of a stone lion set in a retaining wall trickles into a small fountain planted with long-necked calla lilies. Wisteria, dripping from old, thick beams supported on circular brick columns with Doric capitals, shades a sitting area overlooking a panorama of wooded hills and tiled roofs.

A miniature stone elephant in a small round lily pond, opposite, provides an object of contemplation for those lounging on chaises in a glade of gravel. "Grass in the South is difficult to maintain, and you can't put pots on it or you'll have brown spots," says Scheinert. The hands-on gardener pots many flowers, shrubs, and trees because he likes to have the option of moving things around as he fine-tunes his compositions.

Right: Water jets march in single file down the center of a long, terra-cotta-lined canal, adding sound to the charm of an intimate allée focused on a lone iris.

The size and shape of a pool may be debatable, but the axiom for people who entertain outdoors is that there can never be too much deck. The pool may be generously dimensioned for every conceivable recreational and athletic activity, or it may be drop-dead gorgeous. But in many households this small island functions largely as a

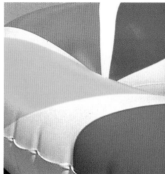

POOLSIDE

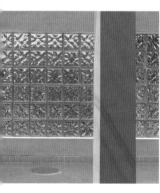

social centerpiece for outdoor living, and hospitality receives a gracious boost when its design is marked by careful planning.

The element of water should be used judiciously, wherever it makes sense within the social context of a house. Close proximity to interior living areas breeds poolside bustle, and the architecture of the house and garden—walls, lighting, plantings—can be designed to draw people outside. A porous facade on a family room—a bank of French doors or sliding glass panels, for example—invites traffic from the house to a deck and pool. A promenade of steps can lead into a hidden garden centered on a pond. If the pool is a satellite in the yard, removed from the house, a secondary structure like a cabana, a pergola, or a loggia encourages a longer stay—especially if it is equipped with a kitchen, a bar, and lounge chairs. A grassy field nearby for touch football, volleyball, or croquet brings more activities into the pool's orbit, enhancing the likelihood that it will become a part of the household's daily rhythm. If it is not conceived as part of a complex of other assets that give the property a multiple nature, the beautiful pool risks becoming an isolated object to be admired only at a distance.

A range of overlapping features helps assure that the pool is not a one-liner but rather an effective social catalyst in its sphere of influence. A barbecue area, shade trellis, wet bar, sound system, exterior lighting, outdoor fireplace, Jacuzzi, built-in seating, and a covey of deck chairs are attractive features that give it added dimension. Underwater ledges built into the sides of pools for casual seating bring the party into the water. A variety of settings—seating clusters, lounging spots, garden enclaves—help turn the outdoor area into an embracing space. Just as a hearth gives an interior room focus, a pool can anchor an outdoor room with its luminous presence.

As a center of home life, the pool and its surrounding amenities offer countless pleasures for the family. But water is a serene substance, one equally suitable for intimate gatherings as for solitary pleasures. You need not dive into the deep end to appreciate its gifts. A pool can be a placid plane of water on which to cast a fishing line or where a child could launch a toy sailboat or a mirror of reflections fascinating to ponder. The pool brims with possibilities.

Page 118: A porticoed pool-house with Doric columns and flowing curtains does double duty as an architectural mask for an unattractive garage located on the neighboring property. The classicized redwood structure, designed by Vincent Jacquart for a house in Hollywood once owned by Bela Lugosi, contains a dressing room, wet bar, steam room, bath, and storage space. Set off by the crisp lines of the angular pool and deck, its stately facade presides augustly over the yard.

Opposite: For his pool area in Palm Springs, Beverly Hills designer Ron Wilson created well-defined seating areas that lure guests outdoors. For one such area, he ensconced chaise longues and a sun umbrella in the curve of a semicircular wall where the existing pool jogs out from the deck. He shaped another by building a covered arcade between the main house and the guest quarters. Lush planting and a pink plaster wash enhance the effect.

Mexican Cool

Not that long ago, under the spreading branches of a centenarian tree, chickens and pigs roamed the sandy backyard of this eightenth-century house in San Miguel de Allende, north of Mexico City. Architect J. B. Johnson and decorator Norman Alfe transformed the property into a working paradise after it was purchased by a Fort Worth, Texas, couple. Outside the kitchen and abutting the living and dining rooms, a lushly planted and potted terrace with ivy-covered persimmon walls frames the vivid hues of the turquoise pool. Larger than most decorative ponds but smaller than average-sized swimming pools, the bright body of water is the centerpiece of a terrace bordered with a loggia—an open but roofed living space furnished for casual alfresco entertaining. The sociability of the patio continues within the pool, where the designers built underwater seats between carved stone gargoyles.

In San Miguel de Allende, American designers J. B. Johnson and Norman Alfe used traditional Mexican materials—stone, mortar, brick, and tile—to give an old Colonial home a pre-Columbian spin. Carved by artisans, stylized horses spilling water into the pool recall mythic Aztec sculptures outside Mexico City and ancient sacrificial pools in the Yucatán.

Peace in Provence

With pieds-à-terre in New York, Marrakech, and Deauville, all created by major design hitters, Pierre Bergé needed a break from architectural glory when he headed to the south of France for some rest and relax-

Cheerful sunflowers set the tone of an outdoor breakfast table under a Provençal arbor planted with grapevines and wisteria for shade, above left and right. One in a series of outdoor rooms, the terrace is paved with a pinkish-gold local stone that is also used for banquettes and as decking around the black-bottomed pool, opposite.

ation. The CEO of Yves Saint Laurent bought an eighteenth-century farmhouse called Mas Théo (after van Gogh's brother) in Saint-Rémy-de-Provence that had no particular architectural distinction, not even a notable garden. Only olive trees left over from the farm occupied the rather sorry grounds. Bergé made the rounds of the local flea markets and antiques stores. Then, with architect Hugues Bosc and landscape designer Michel Sémini, he realized his dream of a modest house

within walking distance of a village. Today it is hard to see the low-lying buildings for the garden: The designers planned the grounds as an informal sequence of outdoor spaces defined by refulgent walls of plants and focused on water. A broad swimming pool lies to the side of the house in one outdoor precinct, and an eighteenth-century demi-lune fountain distinguishes another. But the heart of the house, ringed by all the principal rooms, is the main courtyard centered on an ancient stone basin Bergé transported to the site.

Simple French doors are all that separate Pierre Bergé's bedroom from the adjoining terrace, above. Furnished with unpretentious garden chairs, the outdoor room is shaped by a dense growth of cypress and agapanthus. The main courtyard, left, features an octagonal stone fountain whose soothing sound can be heard throughout the house.

Summer
Stock

For two months every summer, life revolves around the pool in a Sonoma, California, backyard belonging to a television producer. The existing pool, with a Jacuzzi at one semi-circular end and stairs at the other, was not only the centerpiece of the tiny plot but the

In the garden room of the house, above, a convex mirror with a sunburst frame brings the sun indoors even on cloudy days. Upholstered in natural, washable fabrics that accommodate wet bathing suits, the room opens onto a new wood deck overlooking the classically shaped pool, right, which has an underwater seating ledge leading off corner steps.

thematic inspiration for the interiors, done for a client with a well-developed sense of the theatrical. To bring a feeling of summer vacation inside, San Francisco designer Stephen Shubel revamped the interiors of the house and guest quarters. He draped the sitting room with periwinkle-blue oxford cloth to turn the space into a fanciful beach cabana, and then covered all the furniture with oxford cloth, white denim, or white terry cloth for what he calls "an outdoor beachy kind of feeling." A small deck just outside the kitchen was expanded to facilitate informal dinner parties and smooth the transition between house and yard.

Shubel inherited the textured concrete deck around the pool, with a plain but practical exposed aggregate surface that prevents slipping. He furnished the hardscape with chaise longues that can be wheeled into the guesthouse, which doubles as a storage area off-season. The chaises are upholstered in a graphic black-and-white striped water-repellent fabric, Sunbrella, which refuses to fade when left outside. The black piping on the cushions give a tailored look to the casual outdoor setting.

Shubel draped an existing double-gabled gazebo with white denim curtains and furnished it with a wicker table and chairs. White iceberg roses fill terra-cotta pots on the structure's shallow steps and along the edges of the long, narrow lot, which is layered with shrubs and trees to create an opaque wall of greenery.

Calm and Cool

Fisher Vineyards may be located in Sonoma, one of the hottest areas of California, but guests dining alfresco in the gazebo of its private garden are always refreshed by natural air-conditioning. Following the tradition of ancient Persian gardens, San Francisco architects Turnbull Griffin Haesloop deployed water as a coolant. Two swimming pools built on different levels, pinwheeling off either side of the gazebo, create a peninsula effect in which refreshing breezes abound. Connecting the two pools is a concrete channel with a washboard bottom that creates the acoustic effect of a running brook. In addition, the architects piped water up to a trough at the peak of the gable, which overflows onto the roof, spilling down sheets of water that are vaporized by the winds in what is a primitive air-conditioning system. Amid acres of arid vineyards, lush landscaping around the pool gives this microenvironment a verdant quality. With its playful transformations of water, the architects call this folly "a California version of Villa d'Este on the cheap."

A wood-frame gazebo, built like a four-poster bed supporting a simple gable, presides over one of two adjacent pools. With a translucent roof made of inexpensive corrugated fiberglass and semi-decorative framing that functions as an armature for chlorine-resistant plants, the rudimentary structure will mature into a topiary refuge.

Modest Proposal

Pool contractors advised Gep Durenberger that a full-length pool would cost the same as a smaller one, but the antiques dealer chose to go with the petite version so that it would be in scale with the old Spanish Colonial house

The diminutive Spanish Colonial house, above, designed by architect Roy Kelly in 1928, set the tone for the pool. Its terra-cotta roof suggested similar handmade Mexican squares for the deck and pool surround, right, and its muted color inspired an underwater blush made by grinding the clay into the final layer of the pool's plaster lining.

and half-acre San Juan Capistrano, California, garden. "Too many pools dominate the landscape," he says. "I didn't want a pool that would scream at you." What he did want was a water element that would be one of several features in the garden, the most intimate of which is a kitchen patio tucked into an outside corner of the house. The patio faces an old tool shed that was expanded and adapted for lunches, conversation, and bridge. Narrow decks along the sides of the pool lead past a fountain with a life-size terra-cotta statue of Saint Fiacre (goddess of gardens) and on to a large, two-story pavilion at the back of the yard. "The pool serves as the center of the garden's axis," says Durenberger, who intentionally positioned it close to the dressing room so that he could incorporate swimming into his daily routine. To give the yard what he describes as a wonderful sense of privacy, he designed a series of low hedges near the pool "so it would seem somewhat embraced, as though you were in an enclosure rather than on a prairie."

Influenced by Italian garden design, with its emphasis on shade versus sun and openness versus enclosure, Durenberger created a sequence of small, secluded garden alcoves including the cozy kitchen patio near the pool. As in the rest of the garden, simple plant materials are used, especially geraniums, marguerites, and succulents. Modest terra-cotta pots are in keeping with the roof and the floor tiles.

Steeped in Tradition

The hillside properties in Los Angeles that yield the city's fabled views harbor a secret: Their lots are often constricted by the dramatic slopes. The uphill side of the street demands ingenuity and engineering prowess, particularly when a pool figures in the plan. In the Hollywood Hills, Mark Warwick and Kim Hoffman of System Design jimmied a lean black slate pool between a Tuscan-inspired house and a tall, stepped retaining wall. At the south end—where the wall is lowest and the sunlight greatest—they placed a table for outdoor dining.

Warwick and Hoffman evoked the venerability of Mediterranean courtyard houses with an earth-colored palette, crown molding, and stone paving, all orchestrated to give a sense of solidity to the precarious hillside site. The symmetrical design recalls traditional Italian gardens: at one end, a fountain under a Palladian arch; at the other, a small stone obelisk centered between two slender cypress trees.

Color Field

When Charlotte Moss and her husband bought their country house, Boxwood Terrace, on eastern Long Island, the landscaping consisted of little more than a few white pines and some scattered Bradford pears. The long, classically proportioned swimming pool was

Pear trees and urns filled to brimming with helichrysum line the gently sloping bluestone path between the house and the pool, above left. At one end of the pool, a semicircular rose garden flourishes, above right. At the rear of the property, behind teak furniture distinguished by delicate Chinese fretwork, opposite, a trellised fence and wall lattice await climbing plants.

already there, parallel to the main structure, so it became the core of a new, expanded formal garden plan. A devotee of English gardens, Moss envisioned lots of color, but she knew that the garden needed an armature for the anticipated beds and borders. "We wanted axes looking straight out from the living room through the garden that would pull visitors through the yard," she says. To achieve this, she and garden designers Dale Booher and

Lisa Stamm of The Homestead transplanted the pear trees to the sides of the bluestone path between the house and the pool, and plotted rigidly structured borders and flower beds. The existing bluestone deck was expanded for poolside parties, and a low unmortared wall of Pennsylvania fieldstone was built to hold a raised flower border. The result is a pool surrounded by a landscaped room inspired by English garden design—and suffused with a heavenly scent all summer long.

A dry-laid fieldstone wall spotted with alpine plants and broken by a seating alcove supports an exuberant perennial border, above. Densely planted urns mark the corners of the pool, right, and other cardinal points in the formal garden plan.

Overleaf: The view from the house reveals the cumulative effect of a many-layered design strategy—lawns, hedges, borders, and flower beds— serenely centered on the pool.

Flights of Fancy in Malibu

Generally, the path to the pool from Buzz Yudell and Tina Beebe's Mediterranean-style house in Malibu is a fragrant procession past trellised garden rooms, down a flight of steps with a glorious view of the Pacific. But when a party is in full swing, usually around midnight, the promenade becomes the dance floor for an

A broad garden esplanade, above left, steps down one side of the house and past a series of terraced outdoor spaces with panoramic views of the landscape beyond, above right. It culminates in a pool flanked by a canvas-draped pavilion, opposite.

Overleaf: At the base of the steps leading to the pool, night-blooming daturas—the yellow trumpet vine—perfume the air for fragrant after-dinner swims.

exuberant conga line. The couple—he a partner in the Santa Monica architectural firm of Moore Ruble Yudell, she a colorist and garden designer—carefully crafted their house and garden to follow the natural contours of the hills. They chose strong simple shapes to create a series of courtyards and outdoor rooms, defined by pergolas covered with climbing roses or laden with grapevine, that step down a gradual slope leading to the twelve-by-sixty-foot pool and an attendant canvas cabana. "I don't

like to have a pool right next to the house," says Beebe. "I prefer it off in the garden. Then, once you're there, you feel as if you've come to a special place."

When the couple bought the long, narrow property, building codes demanded a driveway wide enough to accommodate a fire truck. Yudell decided to bring the driveway up to the top of the property so that entering the house and walking down its wide side ter-

The outdoor spaces are all paved with Vicenza limestone, a surface that resonates with the rugged Malibu landscape. The covered porch, opposite, overlooks a small lawn planted with white roses. A whirlpool and shower are tucked out of sight in coves just off the terraced staircase.

Just outside the door closest to the kitchen, breakfast is served under a rose-covered trellis, above left, at a low informal table supported by terra-cotta pipes. In the entry courtyard, above right, Iceland poppies push through the cracks in the limestone paving.

race would become a gentle downhill stroll toward the pool. "Looking down at a pool lets you see it as a whole, in the context of the landscape," says Yudell. Dimensioned so that two people can swim side by side, the lap pool still has a deep end. "I wanted it to feel more like a beach, where the color of the water changes with the depth," says Beebe, who tinted the plaster to mimic sand and used unglazed green slate tile at the water line to reinforce the tidal hue.

Compound Structure

The size of the property in the rolling countryside outside New York City, as well as the scale and style of the old Colonial house, suggested a straightforward and generous pool supported by "outbuildings." New York architect James Crisp placed a 25-by-55-foot gunnite pool with a bluestone deck about 150 feet away from the main house. Behind it he added two structures: a white clapboard pool house for the homeowners' two sons, complete with soda fountain, and extra-long built-in beds, and a smaller pitched-roof building to house an in-ground spa. The result is a clean-lined recreational compound tailored to the needs of every family member.

A ceiling fan, above, circulates air around the in-ground spa in one of the two outbuildings. Outside, right, the pool features atypical details: straight rather than bullnosed coping and right-angled rather than radial corners, and the bluestone deck is set in stone dust, a crushed rock coarser than sand and with more give than concrete.

Untamed in L.A.

An ink-drop pool straight from the 1950s came with the Los Angeles house bought by an avid gardener and her husband. Despite its organic shape, the pool didn't have the Romantic naturalism the homeowners desired. To make the form more irregular, architect Mark Rios, who collaborated with his partner, Charles Pearson, and garden designer Pat

Against the deep blue of the lagoon-like pool, above, plants are massed in dense bunches rather than arranged to form distinct geometric shapes. Tenacious mosses growing between the stones, right, enhance the unruly effect.

Holland, cut through sections of the coping, eliminating part of the undistinguished concrete deck and integrating the pool and terrace into a yard reconceived as a landscape. "We tried to blur the outline of the pool by removing the deck from the edge and bringing plant material up to the water," says Rios. The garden now looks more haphazard. The exuberant plants are high, thick, and tangled enough to assume the foreground, while the pool and the house, normally the dominant features of a landscape, are virtually submerged.

Flagstone walls disappearing below the waterline suggest a natural pool of water caught among shelves of stratified rock, left. Boulders imported to the site and scattered throughout the overgrowth tumble over the stone ledge. Painted metal dining furniture, above, fills in a bald spot in this backyard thicket, where the natural is allowed to overwhelm the man-made.

Stacking Up

In a Miami Shores house designed for her parents, architects Laurinda Spear and Bernardo Fort-Brescia subverted the typical suburban expectations of the backyard pool by stacking pool, yard, garage, and rooms within one long, slender structure that has the concision of a town house. Building the pool up from grade, they created an elevated

courtyard designed as an outdoor living room. The strategy of absorbing the outdoor spaces within the body of the house allows the interiors to open onto the pool deck for a strong indoor-outdoor relationship.

Glass bricks in the front wall admit light but afford privacy, left. A fixed canvas awning shelters a table for outdoor dining. Five different shades of pink, above, shape the architectural forms and accentuate the effect of perceived depth around the pool.

A Pool for All Seasons

For a Chicago couple who wanted to do most of their summer entertaining poolside, architect Evan LeDuc approached the design of their Michigan retreat strategically. The pool was sited next to the barn to add importance to the former outbuilding, which was converted into a combination guesthouse and pool house. Coupling the pool with the voluminous building gives the property a large-scale entertainment space that would have been difficult to develop around the small main house. LeDuc paid special attention to the dimensions of the pool, creating large decks at each end and generous ten-foot-wide runs along the sides. The whole design is simple and abstract, to complement the wooded landscape and grass. "The earth rolls between the house and the barn, and when you're in the pool the lawn drops off, so you feel you're floating in the landscape," the architect explains.

Michigan summers can produce very intense heat. To minimize its blistering effect around the pool, the architect used Cool Deck, a concrete with pulverized marble added to the mix. The deck is simply furnished with unpainted chaise longues, a capacious canvas parasol, and terra-cotta pots exuberantly brimming with red geraniums. To deal with the other end of the weather spectrum, a rigid cover is used to resist heavy snow loads.

Into the Woods

he Hamptons vacation house that has been Alfredo De Vido's personal work in progress for many years is based on a wood aesthetic, from the paneled interiors to the shingle siding and the expansive cedar deck. The New York architect lived in Japan for three years and worked in Scandinavia for several more, "so wood is in my background," he says. The woods make the modern prismatic forms of his home friendlier to the eye and the touch, and ingratiate the architecture with the surrounding landscape, which is distinguished by a stand of white pines he has groomed for years. He sited the swimming pool on an axis with the principal opening into the living room, and at the far end of the axis he built a trellised pergola seamlessly integrated within the grove—"a good spot for lunch," he explains. The black-bottomed pool is only one of a half dozen water features on the property that are spatially defined by fencing, planting, and terracing.

Built-in planters and movable wooden boxes filled with white geraniums surround the cedar deck. A berm of mountain laurels climbing over a change of levels behind the lightweight deck chairs separates the pool from an adjacent outdoor room.

The trellised roof scape of the dining gazebo perched in a grove of mature white pines, above, echoes the structure of the main house. The woodland scene is beautifully reflected on the surface of the black-bottomed vinyl pool. On an axis with the master bedroom is a small fishpond, opposite, animated by a short jet of water. For a "natural" garden that wouldn't require extensive care in the area's acidic soil, De Vito limited his palette of plants to hardy irises, day lilies, and wild geraniums for the perimeter of the pond.

Not So Simple Pleasures

When New York landscape architect Edmund Hollander remodeled an existing 1960s pool on an East Hampton estate, he simply squared it off into a pure rectangle. But simplicity is deceiving within the white picket fence. The pool, which allows plenty of room for laps, is also equipped for lounging with two 24-inch-wide steps at the shallow end and an underwater bench at the deep end, simultaneously encouraging kids and adults to swim and relax. What appears to be a regular deck is subtly varied for different uses: The far, gently curved side is wide enough for chairs and dining, while the other end is sized for a pergola attached to a pool house. Patterned with small and large squares of bluestone interlocked in a random pattern, the deck is cooled on hot summer days by discreetly placed irrigation heads. Flanking the pool, a wide expanse of grass is bordered by an old-fashioned palette of flowers, including lavender, peonies, climbing roses, lilies, and hollyhocks.

A fence inspired by architectural details from the 1890s Shingle-Style house encircles the pool area, making a sliding cover unnecessary. With walls tinted a medium to dark gray, the pool, which is left uncovered in winter, looks like a reflecting pond.

Directory of Designers and Architects

Jan Abell
Abell-Garcia Architects
Tampa, Fla.
(813) 251-3652

Paul Aferiat
Stamberg/Aferiat
Architecture
New York, N.Y.
(212) 255-4173

James Aman
Chatham, N.J.
(973) 701-9306

Leslie Armstrong
Armstrong Associates
New York, N.Y.
(212) 353-4830

Gae Aulenti
Milan, Italy
(011 39) 25-280-2613

Tina Beebe
Moore, Ruble +Yudell
Santa Monica, Calif.
(310) 450-1400

Barry Beer
Barry Beer Design
Los Angeles, Calif.
(310) 204-6228

Barry Berkus
B3 Architects/Berkus
Design Studio
Santa Barbara, Calif.
(805) 966-1547

David Birn
New York, N.Y.
(914) 265-2450

Dale Booher
The Homestead
Shelter Island Heights, N.Y.
(516) 749-2189

Hugues Bosc
Saint-Rémy-de-Provence,
France
(011 33) 16-90-92-1081

Suby Bowden
Suby Bowden +Architects
LLC
Santa Fe, N.Mex.
(505) 983-3755

Thomas Callaway
Thomas Callaway &
Associates
Santa Monica, Calif.
(310) 828-1030

Anne Carson
Aman & Carson, Inc.
New York, N.Y.
(212) 794-8878

Jack DeBartolo, Jr.
DeBartolo Architects
Phoenix, Ariz.
(602) 264-6617

Alfredo De Vido
Alfredo De Vido Architects
New York, N.Y.
(212) 517-6100

Joe D'Urso
East Hampton, N.Y.
(516) 329-3634

Mary Dial
Mary Dial Design
Clayton, N.Y.
(315) 686-2789

Gep Durenberger
Le Sueur, Minn.
(507) 665-6855

David Anthony Easton
New York, N.Y.
(212) 334-3820

Steven Ehrlich
Steven Ehrlich Architects
Culver City, Calif.
(310) 838-9700

Bernardo Fort-Brescia
Arquitectonica (ARQ)
Miami, Fla.
(305) 372-1812

Pierre François
Saint-Tropez, France
(011 33) 949-78089

Kenneth Garcia
Abell-Garcia Architects
Tampa, Fla.
(813) 251-3652

Eric Haesloop
Turnbull Griffin Haesloop
San Francisco, Calif.
(415) 986-3642

Kelly Harmon
Kelly Harmon Interiors &
Design
Los Angeles, Calif.
(310) 230-6716

Mark Harwick
The System Design
Beverly Hills, Calif.
(310) 556-7711

David Hicks
London, England
(011 44) 1-71-734-3183

Kim Hoffman
The System Design
Beverly Hills, Calif.
(310) 556-7711

Edmund D. Hollander
Edmund D. Hollander
Design
New York, N.Y.
(212) 473-0620

Philetus H. Holt III
Holt, Morgan, Russell
Architects
Princeton, N.J.
(609) 924-1358

Hugh Newell Jacobsen
Washington, D.C.
(202) 337-5200

Vincent Jacquart
Hollywood, Calif.
(213) 850-8241

Raymond Jungles
Key West, Fla.
(305) 296-5312

Bruno Lafourcade &
Dominique Lalande
Saint Rémy-de-Provence,
France
(011 33) 49-092-1014

Evan LeDuc
Development Services
Benton Harbor, Mich.
(616) 849-3509

James Light
Mallory James Interiors
Portland, Maine
(207) 773-0180

Hitch Lyman
Trumansburg, N.Y.
(607) 272-8165

Mallory Marshall
Mallory James Interiors
Portland, Maine
(207) 773-0180

Lionel Morrison
Morrison Seifert Murphy
Dallas, Tex.
(214) 651-0700

Steve Martino
Steve Martino &
Associates
Phoenix, Ariz.
(602) 957-6150

J. D. Morrow
J. D. Morrow & Associates
Architects
Santa Fe, N.Mex.
(505) 988-1559

Jeffrey D. Mose
Mose Associates Architects
Ridgefield, Conn.
(203) 438-5355

Charlotte Moss
Charlotte Moss & Co.
New York, N.Y.
(212) 772-6244

Elie Mouyal
Amerchiche Marrakech,
Morocco
(011 212) 430-0603

Brian Alfred Murphy
BAM Construction/Design,
Inc.
Santa Monica, Calif.
(310) 459-0955

Ben Page
Ben Page & Associates
Nashville, Tenn.
(615) 320-0220

Charles Pearson
Santa Fe, N.Mex
(505) 983-4815

Nancy Goslee Power
Santa Monica, Calif.
(310) 394-0261

Mark Rios
Rios Associates
Los Angeles, Calif.
(323) 852-6717

Michel Sémini
Goult, France
(011 33) 4-90-72-2752

Stephen Shubel
Stephen Shubel Design
Ross, Calif.
(415) 925-9332

Paul Siskin
Siskin Valls, Inc.
New York, N.Y.
(212) 752-3790

Laurinda Spear
Arquitectonica (ARQ)
Miami, Fla.
(305) 372-1812

Peter Stamberg
Stamberg/Aferiat
Architecture
New York, N.Y.
(212) 255-4173

Lisa Stamm
The Homestead
Shelter Island Heights, N.Y.
(516) 749-2189

Jack Staub
Hortulus Farm
Wrights Town, Penn.
(215) 598-0660

Turnbull Griffin Haesloop
San Francisco, Calif.
(415) 986-3642

Lynn von Kersting
Indigo Seas
Los Angeles, Calif.
(310) 550-8758

Mark Warwick
The System Design
Beverly Hills, Calif.
(310) 556-7711

Ron Wilson
Ron Wison Designers
Bererly Hills, Calif.
(310) 276-0666

Jacques and Peter Wirtz
Wirtz International
Schoten, Belgium
(011 323) 680-1322

Debra Yates
Key West, Fla.
(305) 296-5312

Buzz Yudell
Moore Ruble Yudell
Santa Monica, Calif.
(310) 450-1400

Photography Credits

1	Thibault Jeanson
2	Ken Druse
4	Cookie Kinkead
6	Scott Frances
8	Tim Street-Porter
10	Joshua Greene
12	Judith Watts
15–19	Tim Street-Porter
20–22	Oberto Gili
24	Christopher Irion
26–27	Timothy Hursley
28–31	Antoine Bootz
32–35	Robert Lautman
36–43	Tim Street-Porter
44–47	Robert Lautman
48–51	John Hall
52–55	Norman McGrath
56–58	Scott Frances
60	Richard Felber
63–67	John Hall
68–75	Richard Felber
76–79	John Vaughan
80	Peter Aaron/Esto
82–83	Jack Winston
84–89	Alexandre Bailhache
90–91	Richard Felber
92–95	Curtice Taylor
96–97	Dominique Vorillon
98–101	William Waldron
102–105	Alexandre Bailhache
106–107	Tim Street-Porter & Kathlene Persoff
108–111	Dana Hyde
112–117	Alexandre Bailhache
118	Cookie Kinkead
121	Elyse Lewin
122	Tim Street-Porter
124–127	Oberto Gili
128–131	Jon Jensen
132	Cookie Kinkead
134–137	John Vaughan
138	Patrick House
140–145	Rob Gray
146–151	John Vaughan
152	Judith Watts
154–159	Tim Street-Porter
160	John Vaughan
162–165	Judith Watts
166	Thibault Jeanson
168	Paul Warchol
171	Cookie Kinkead
173	Tim Street-Porter
174	William Waldron
176	Jeremy Samuelson